HOW DO WAVES BEHAVE? HOW ARE THEY MEASURED?

Physics Lessons for Kids
Children's Physics Books

Speedy Publishing LLC

40 E. Main St. #1156

Newark, DE 19711

www.speedypublishing.com

Copyright 2017

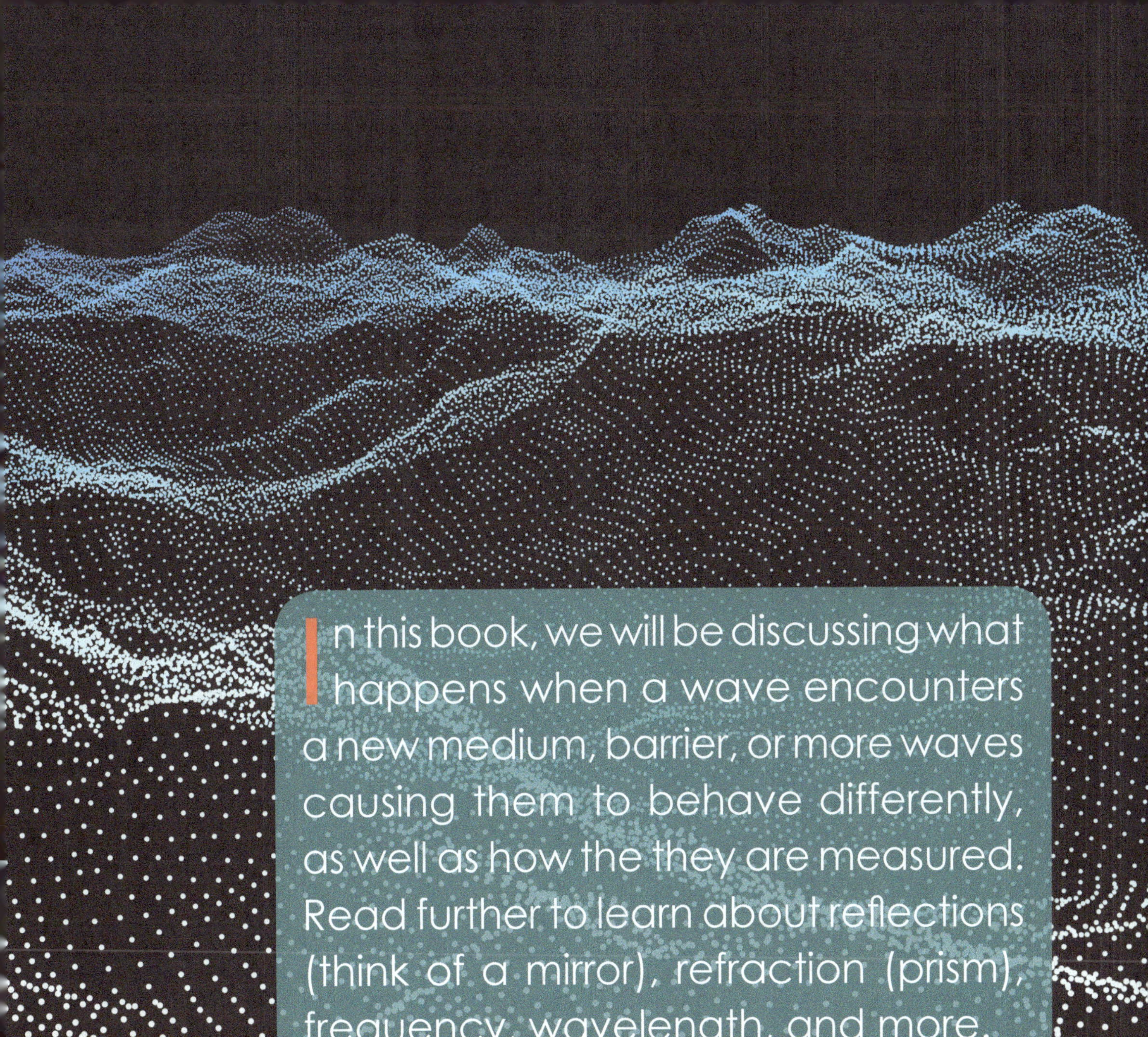
In this book, we will be discussing what happens when a wave encounters a new medium, barrier, or more waves causing them to behave differently, as well as how the they are measured. Read further to learn about reflections (think of a mirror), refraction (prism), frequency, wavelength, and more.

HOW DO WAVES BEHAVE?

REFLECTION

We use "reflection" in life when describing what we observe as we look at a mirror or the water's surface.

GIRL LOOKING AT HER REFLECTION IN THE MIRROR

STREET-SPHERE-MIRROR

In the world of physics, a reflection is the result of a wave encountering a new medium acting as a barricade, which causes it to return to the first medium. It then "reflects" at an angle off the barrier, incidental to the wave's angle, as it hits the barrier.

REFRACTION

A wave refraction occurs when it changes direction as it moves from one medium to another medium. As the direction changes, refraction will also cause a length change as well as a change to the wave's speed. The amount of this change resulting from refraction depends upon the mediums' refractive index.

REFRACTION THROUGH A GLASS

RAY OF LIGHT REFRACTING

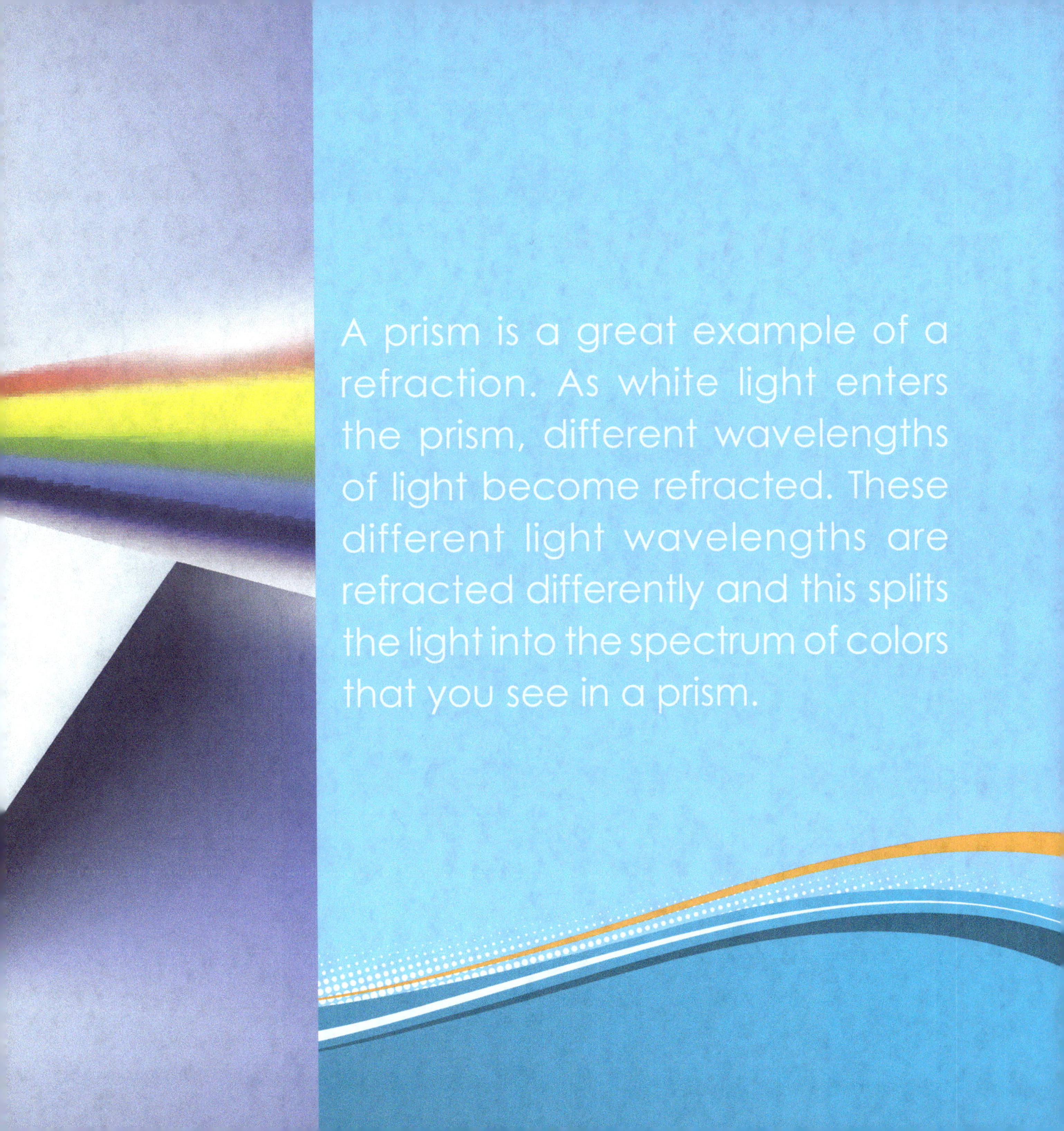

A prism is a great example of a refraction. As white light enters the prism, different wavelengths of light become refracted. These different light wavelengths are refracted differently and this splits the light into the spectrum of colors that you see in a prism.

DIFFRACTION

When waves stay in the same medium, but bend around an obstacle, this is known as diffraction. This occurs as a wave comes into contact with a small object that is in its way, or when it is forced to go through a tiny opening. An example would be when a wave of water hits a boat and moves the boat around. The waves that follow the boat are diffracted (changed).

DIFFRACTION OF WAVES

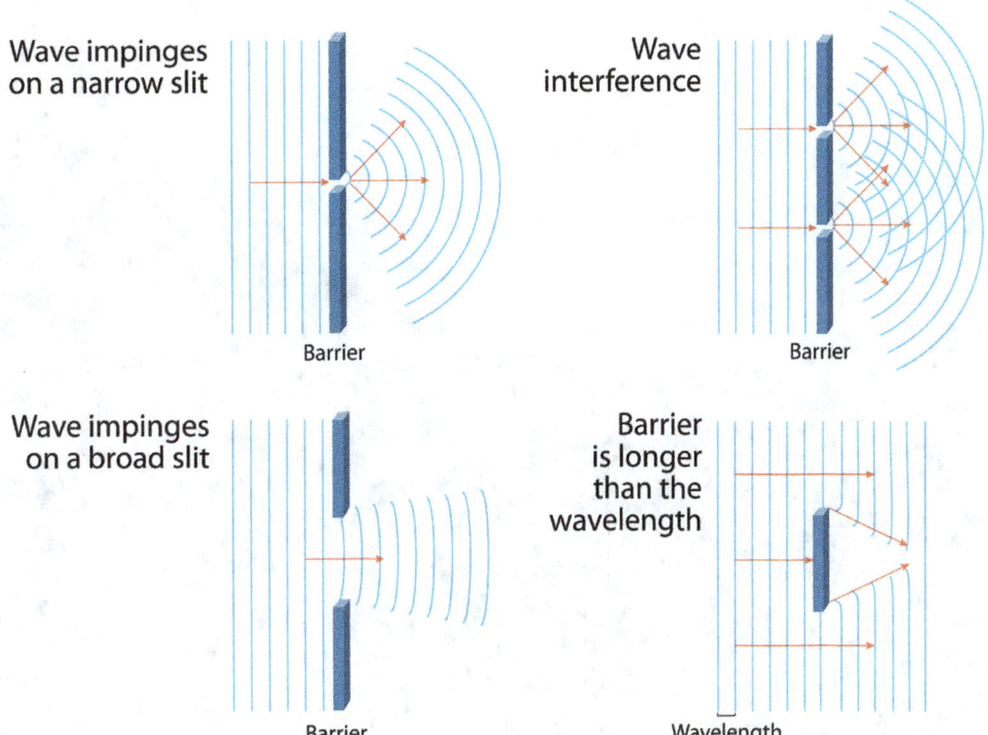

POLARIZING FILTER FOR CAMERA LENS

POLARIZATION

Polarization occurs as a wave oscillates in one direction. Often, light waves are polarized by use of a polarizing filter. The only ones that are able to be polarized are transverse waves. Longitudinal waves, including sound waves, are not able to be polarized since they will always be traveling in the same direction as the wave is traveling.

ABSORPTION

When a wave comes in contact with a medium, causing the molecules in the medium to move and vibrate, this is known as absorption. The vibration is able to take, or absorb, some energy from it, causing less energy to reflected.

SOUND ABSORPTION MATERIAL

Black pavement absorbs energy from the light, making it a great example of absorption. The pavement gets hot from absorption of light waves, and only a small amount of light is reflected and the pavement appears black. The white stripe you often see painted on the pavement reflects more light and absorbs less light, and will not be as hot as the black pavement.

INTERFERENCE

Interference occurs as one wave comes in contact with a second one. As they meet, the resulting wave has the amplitude which is the sum of the two interfering waves.

TWO WAVES INTERFERING

constructive interference

destructive interference

wave peak comes upon wave peak

wave peak comes upon wave trough

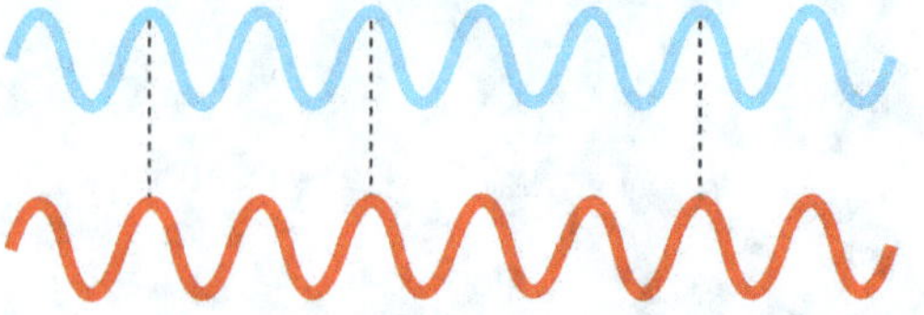

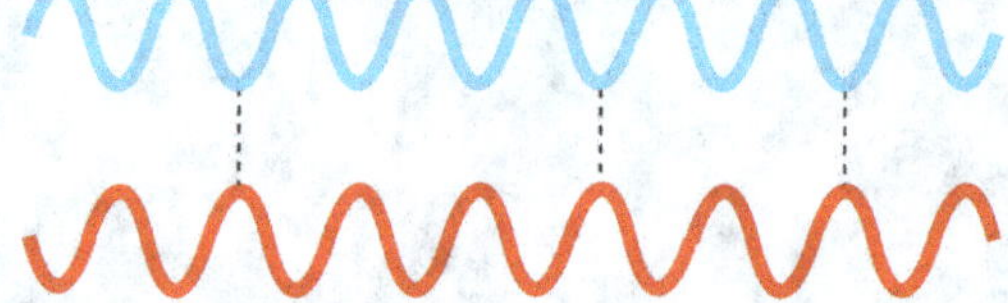

Interference can be destructive or constructive, dependent upon the waves' phase. When the resulting wave has a higher amplitude over the interfering waves, this is referred to as constructive interference. If its amplitude is lower, it is known as destructive interference.

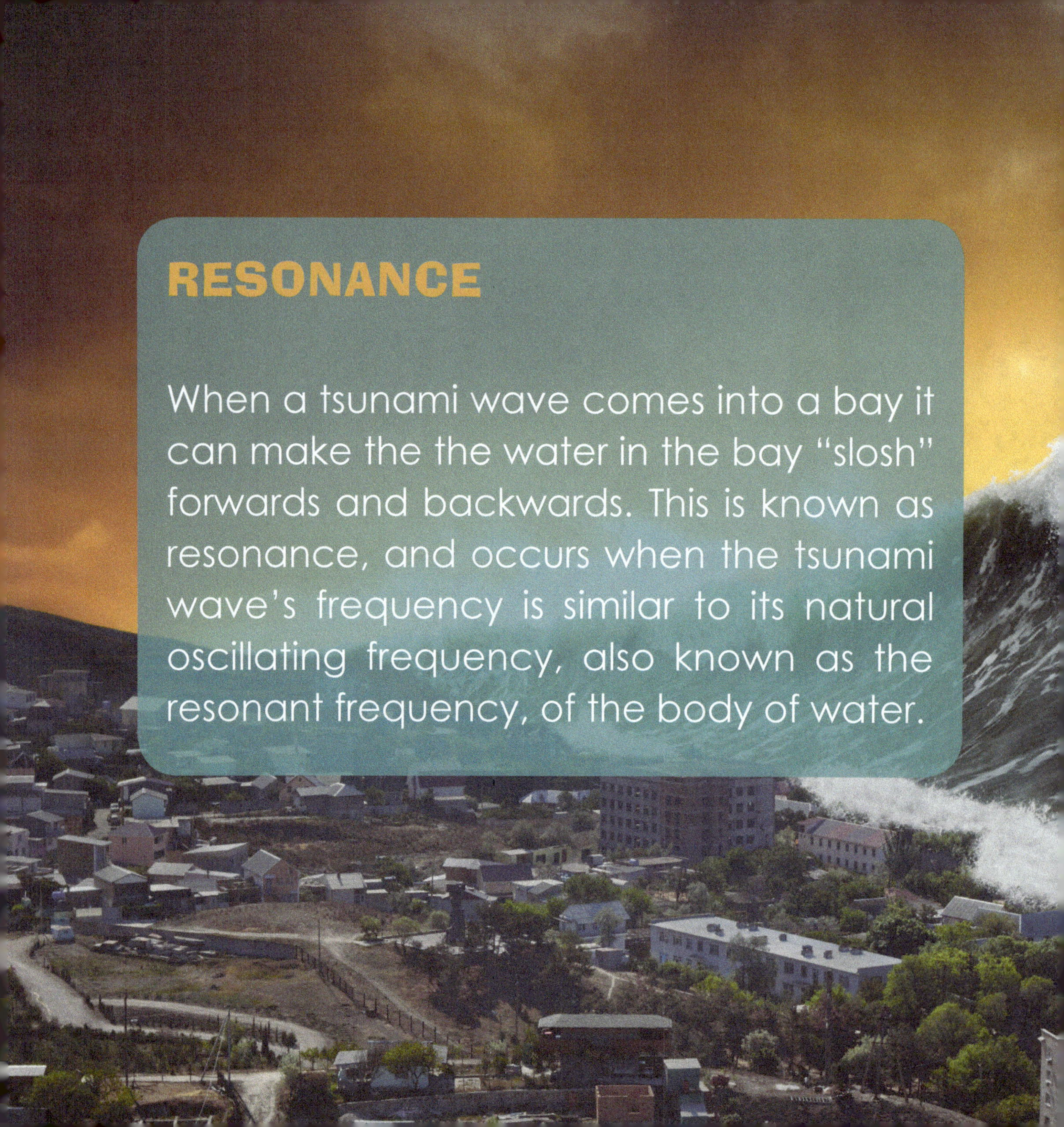

RESONANCE

When a tsunami wave comes into a bay it can make the the water in the bay "slosh" forwards and backwards. This is known as resonance, and occurs when the tsunami wave's frequency is similar to its natural oscillating frequency, also known as the resonant frequency, of the body of water.

TSUNAMI

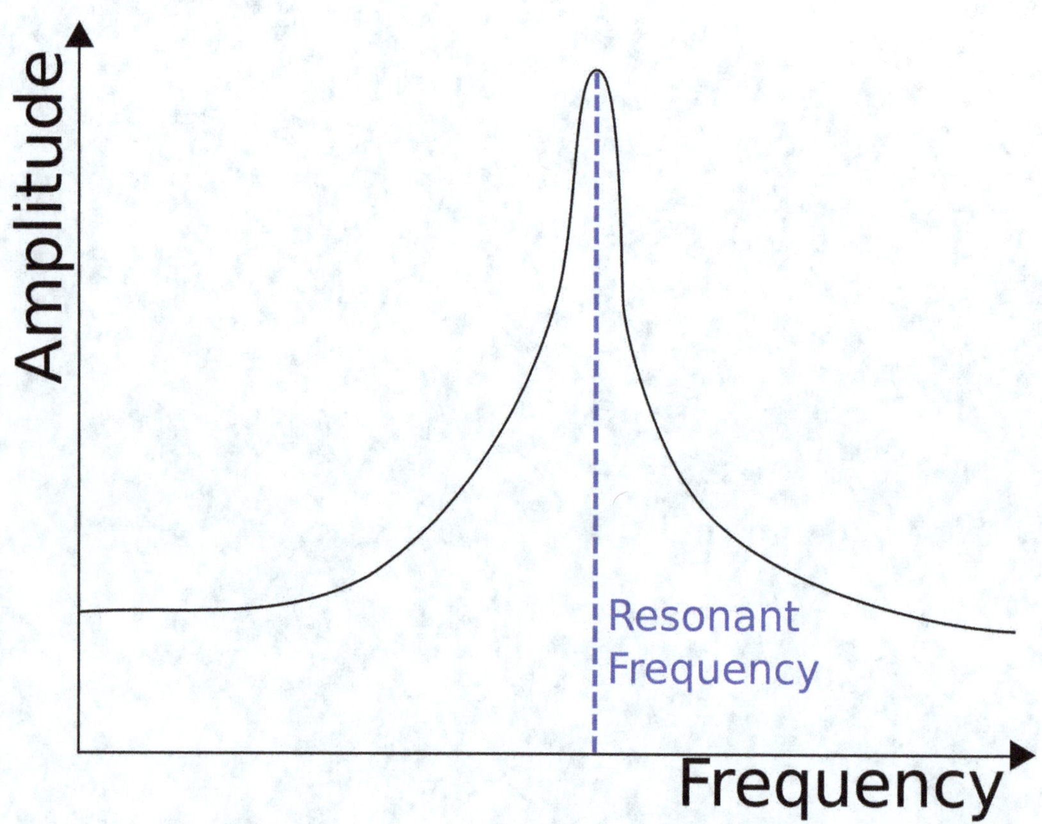

Amplitude
Frequency
Resonant
Frequency

The resonance pushes the level of the water extremely high which makes the tsunami effect greater. The size and shape of the body of water will create various resonant frequencies.

HOW ARE THEY MEASURED?

SPEED

The measure of how quickly a wave travels is known as the wave speed. Its calculation is the ratio of the distance it travels to the amount of time it takes for it to travel that particular distance.

SPEED BOAT RUNNING IN THE SEA

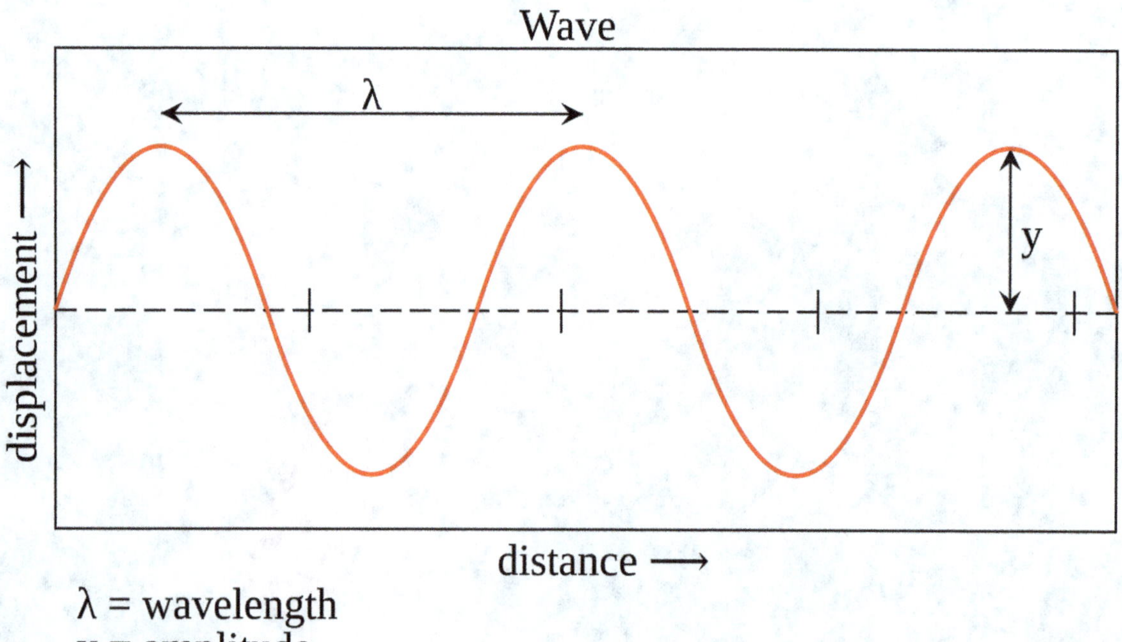

Wave
λ
displacement
y
distance
λ = wavelength
y = amplitude

The wave's speed can be calculated if you know the frequency, period and wavelength. Its speed is calculated as the ration of one period of the wave to one wavelength of it. It also is calculated to be the product of the frequency and the wavelength.

If the frequency or the wavelength is increased, the speed of the waves is also increased. In some waves such as light, the speed will remain constant in any given medium, as one of the variables is increased (wavelength) this will cause the other variable (frequency) to decrease.

LIGHT WAVE

WAVE ON OSCILLOSCOPE

FREQUENCY

Frequency is the measurement of the number of cycles occurring during a certain time period, i.e. cycles per second. If a motor turns 50 revolutions per second, it is considered to have a frequency of 50 Hertz. Hertz is abbreviated as Hz, and is named for Heinrich Hertz, who was a member of the Hertz family known for their significant contributions to the world of physics. Frequency appears as the letter "f" in formulas.

WAVELENGTH

The property that people can find easily and quickly is a wavelength. This is used to tell them apart. The parts of a wave that points up similar to a mountain are referred to as crests. Parts that slope down similar to a valley are called troughs. A wavelength is defined as being the distance from a certain height on a wave to the next place on it being the same height and traveling in the same direction.

AMATEUR BAND
MOTALA
BOSTON
CHUNGKING
SPAIN
S.W.1
S.W.2
LONG WAVE
SELECTIVITY
K.C.
BROAD
LOCAL
SHARP
DISTANT
MIN TREBLE
TREBLE CONTROL
PRAGUE
KALUNDB'G
WARSAW I
LUXEMB'G
OSLO
LIGHT PROG
METRES
1200
1000
800
1400
1600
1800
2000
MOTALA
REYKJAVIK
MOSCOW I
ALLOUIS
BRASOV
LONG WAVE
AIRCRAFT
S.W.2
DYNATRON
THE SUPREME REPRODUCER
MODEL T.69
WAVE CHANGE
GRAM.
L.W.
M.W.
S.W.2
S.W.
TUNING DIAL

Wavelengths are typically measured in meters. There doesn't have to be a certain spot to start at for measuring the wavelength, however, you will need to make sure it is traveling in the same direction and it is the same height. Typically, people prefer measuring from one crest to the next one, or from trough to trough, only since they are easier to spot.

The wavelength on a longitudinal wave measures from the middle of two compressions or two expansions. As the molecules move from left to right they cause the wave and the disturbance to travel in the same direction. When the molecules are bunched together this is known as a compression. When the molecules are spread out this is known as a rarefaction.

Waveforms

Transverse Wave

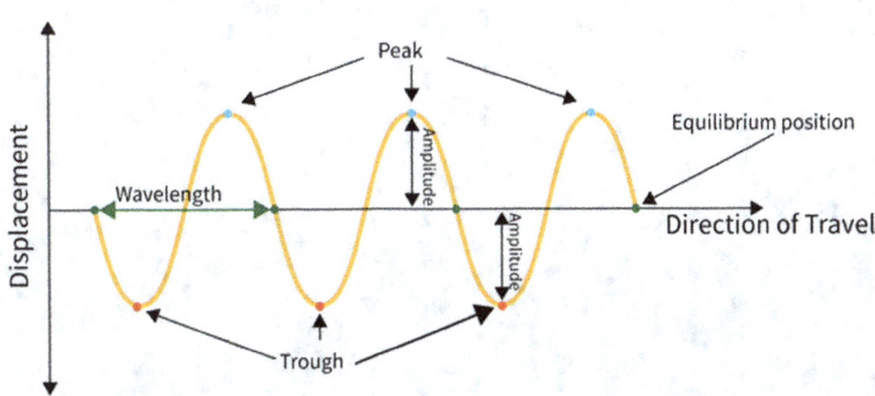

Longitudinal Wave

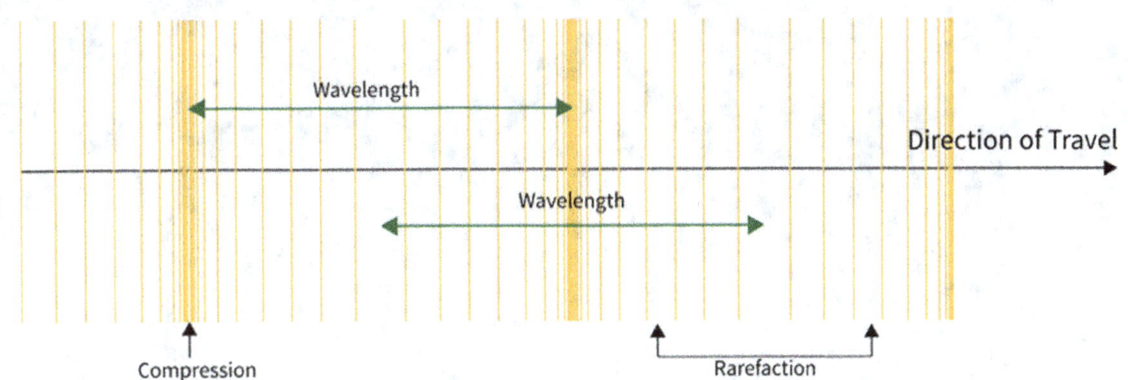

The two most important formulas used when studying waves are:

- Frequency is the number of waves that pass a certain point per second, inverse of time.

- Wavelength is the length of waves, similar to a displacement, and measured in meters.

- Multiplying these together, which is multiplying 1/s and m, giving us m/s, equals the wave's velocity.

AMPLITUDE

The measurement of a wave's size is known as its amplitude.

Think about an ocean wave. It might be a giant tsunami or a small ripple. What you are really visioning are waves that have various amplitudes. They may have the same wavelength and frequency, but their amplitudes can vary greatly.

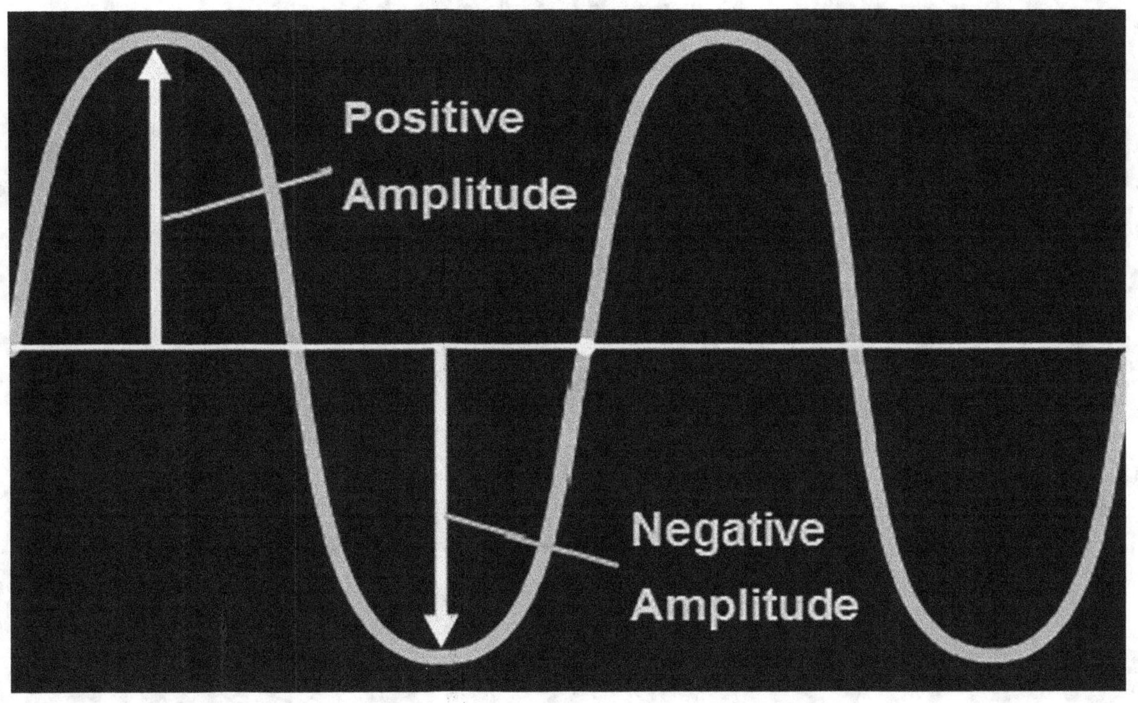
Positive
Amplitude
Negative
Amplitude

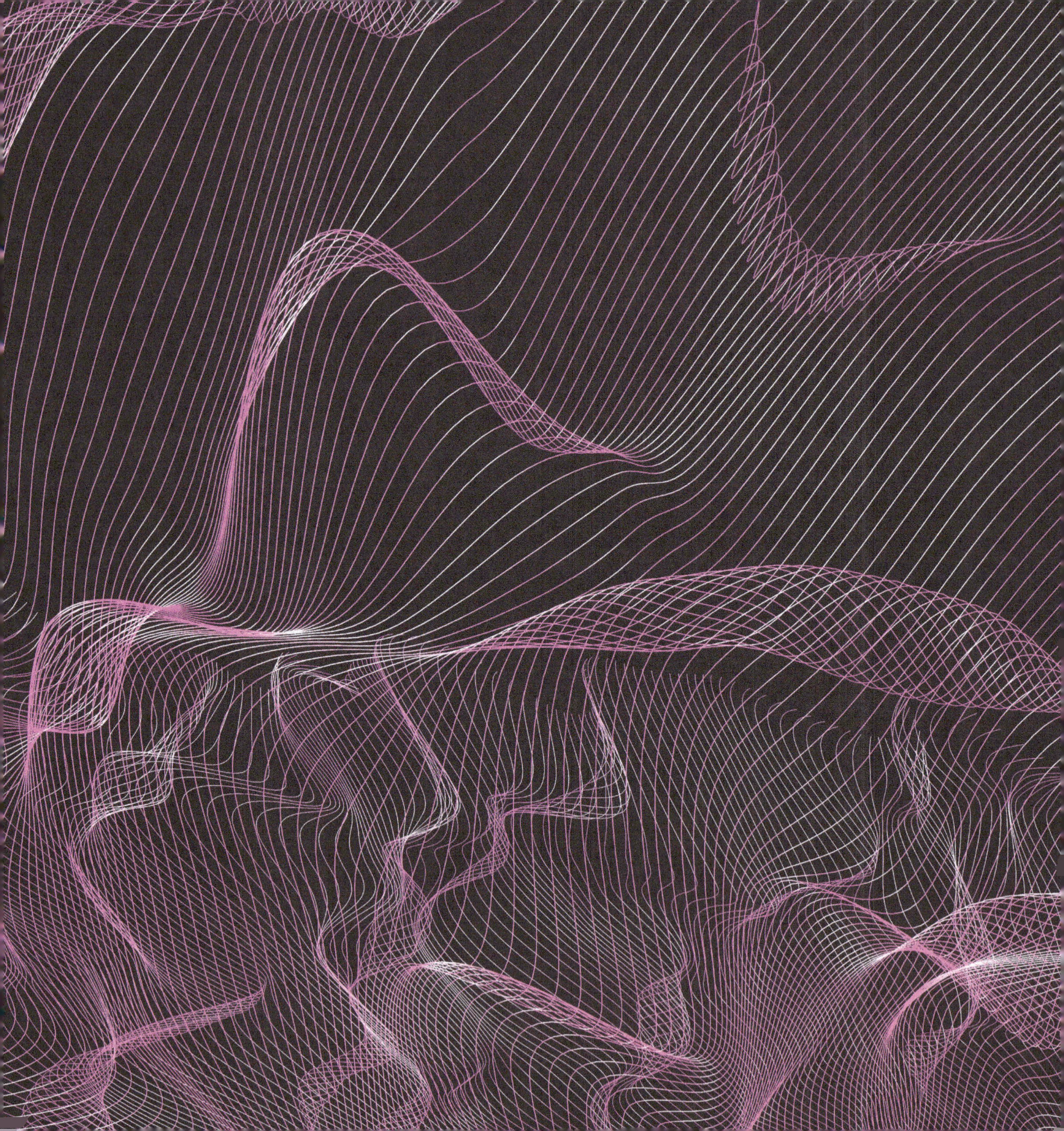

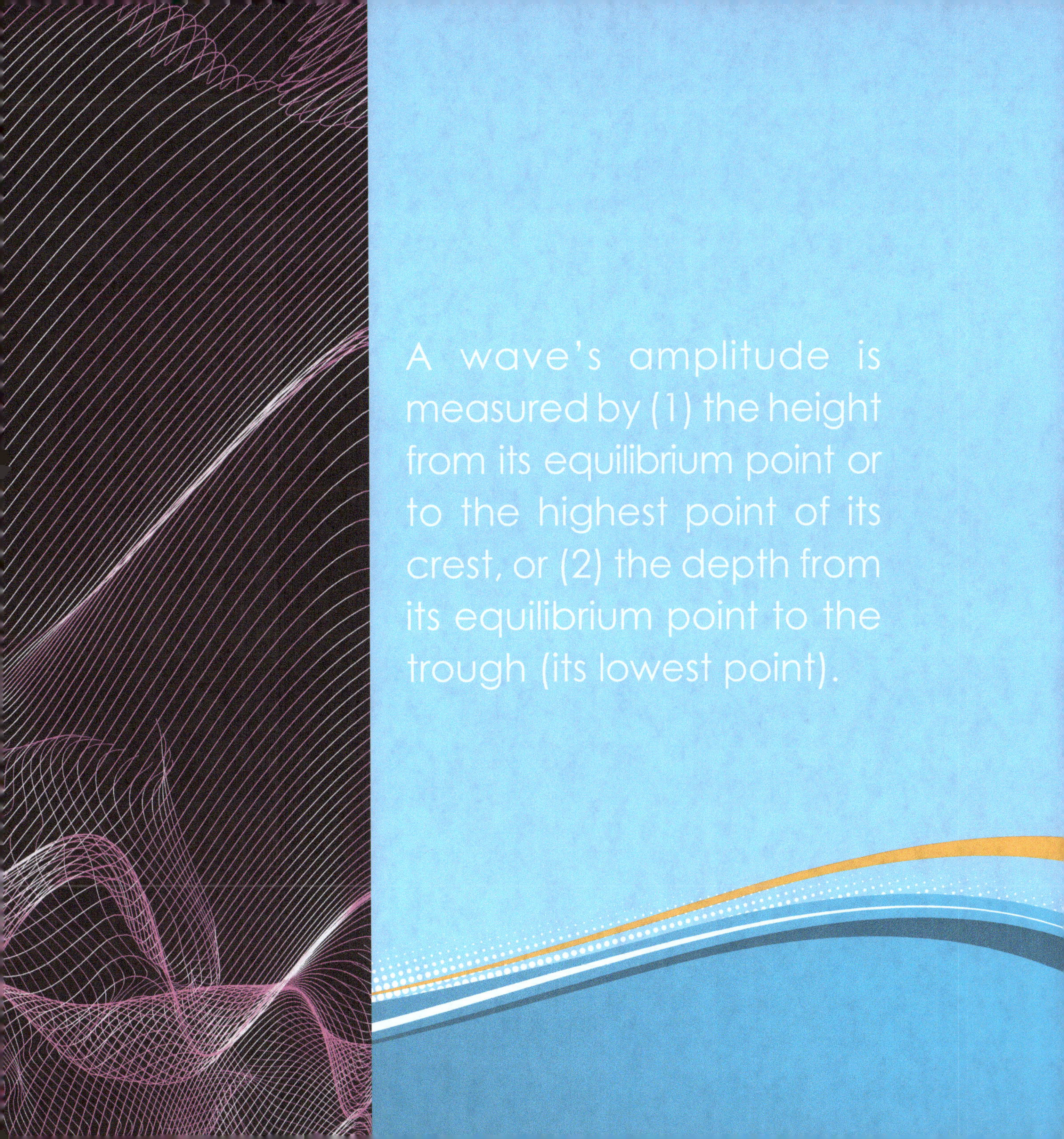

A wave's amplitude is measured by (1) the height from its equilibrium point or to the highest point of its crest, or (2) the depth from its equilibrium point to the trough (its lowest point).

When measuring the wave's amplitude, we are actually watching the wave's energy.

- ➲ It requires additional energy in order to make a greater amplitude wave.

- ➲ When you want to remember this, think about an amplifier for a home stereo that makes the amplitude larger by using additional electrical energy.

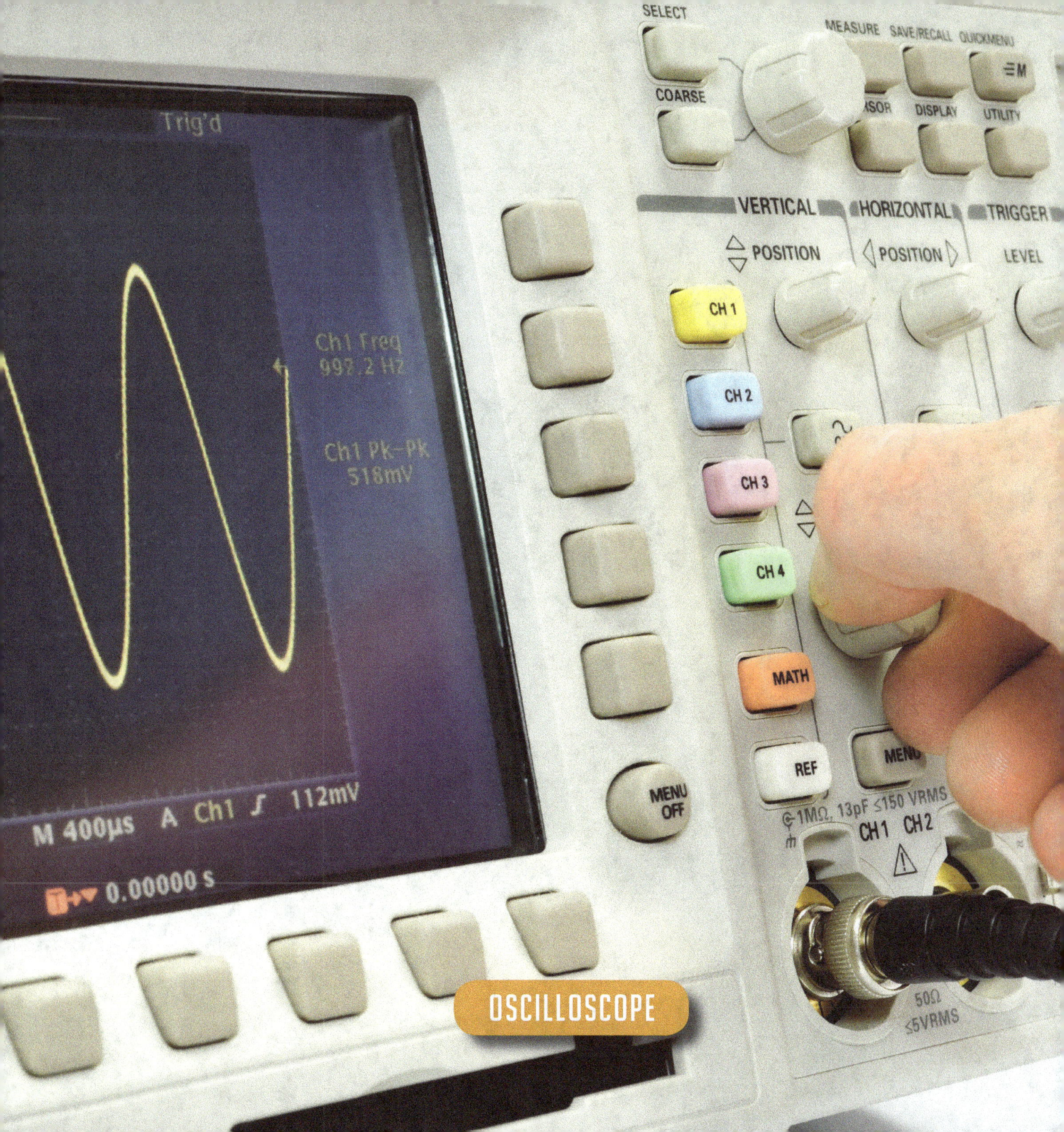

Trig'd
Ch1 Freq
997.2 Hz
Ch1 Pk-Pk
518mV
M 400µs   A Ch1   112mV
0.00000 s
SELECT
COARSE
MEASURE SAVE/RECALL QUICKMENU
≡M
CURSOR DISPLAY UTILITY
VERTICAL
HORIZONTAL
TRIGGER
POSITION
POSITION
LEVEL
CH 1
CH 2
CH 3
CH 4
MATH
REF
MENU
MENU
OFF
1MΩ, 13pF ≤150 VRMS
CH 1   CH 2
50Ω
≤5VRMS
OSCILLOSCOPE

GIRL BALANCING ON SURF BOARD

WAVE PERIOD

Have you seen someone surfing or tried it yourself? There have to be waves for surfing, but not just any wave. Surfers are looking to catch a wave that is big and nice, or has a high amplitude. It won't be enjoyable if it appears and disappears right away. They like to ride waves that last a long time, or have a long wavelength or wave period.

All waves, including ocean waves, have peaks or crests, which are its highest points. Each wave will also have troughs, which are their lowest points. As discussed earlier, the wavelength is the distance between one crest and the next crest.

OCEAN WAVES

The distance from one peak to the next peak is the same distance between one trough and the next trough. The wavelength can also be measured from one trough to the next one. In either instance, the wavelength measures the distance of one completion of the wave's pattern, going up and down, otherwise known as the wave cycle.

The amount of time taken for the wave cycle to complete is known as the wave period. The wave period is represented by the letter "T" and is measured in seconds.

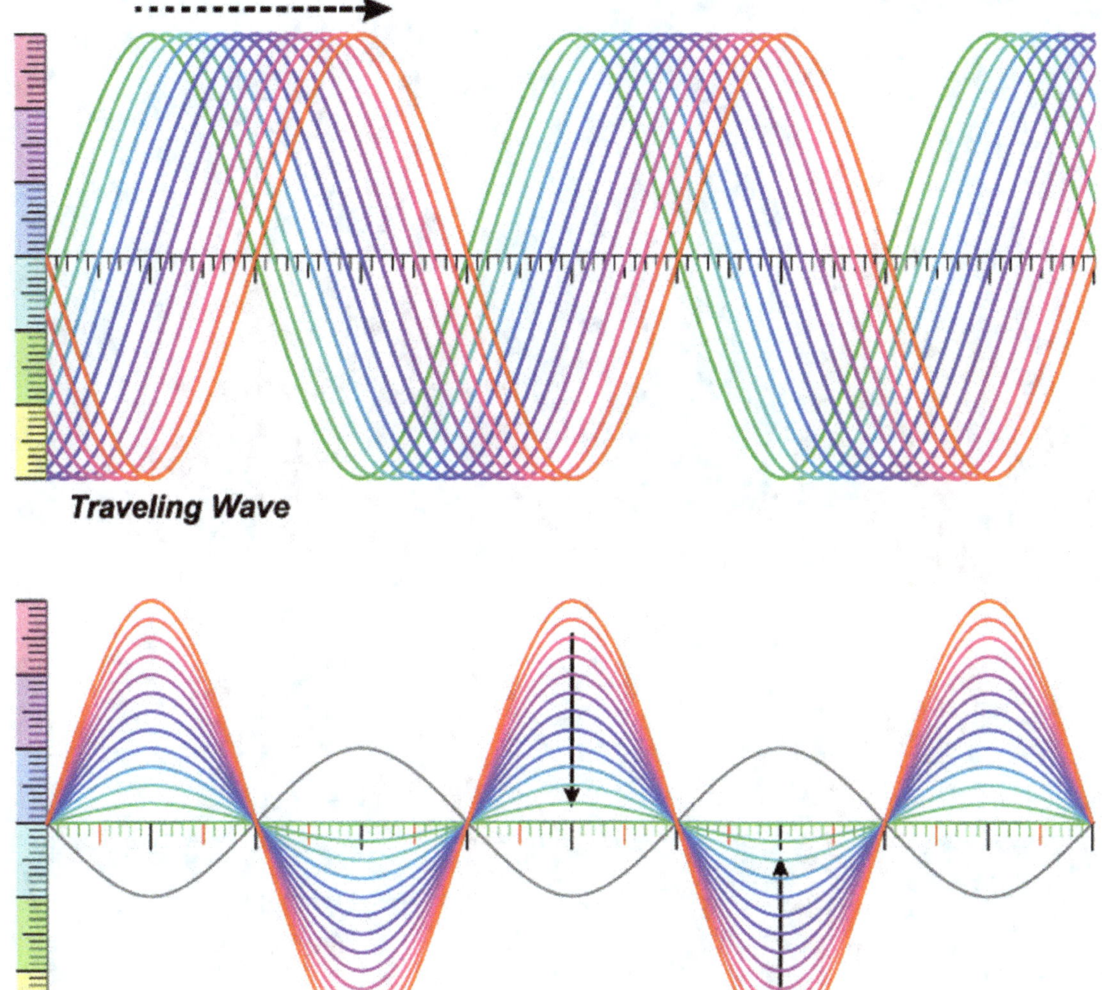

Traveling Wave
Standing Wave

Now that you have learned more about waves and how they are measured and their parts, think about using this information in everyday life. One project might be to research ocean waves on the internet and when you look at the waves, think about what the crest is, what a trough is, and what its amplitude is.

For additional information about waves as used in the world of physics, you can go to your local library, research the internet and ask your science teachers!

Visit
BABY PROFESSOR
EDUCATION KIDS
www.BabyProfessorBooks.com
to download Free Baby Professor eBooks and view
our catalog of new and exciting Children's Books